WHAT ARE PEOPLE SAYING?!

"Funnier than two drunk Irishmen at Fagan's Pub."
—*Saint Patrick*

"If I had known he was this good I would have booked him on the Ark."
—*Noah*

"He nailed it tonight, which is a good thing. He had some trouble nailing it as a carpenter."
—*Joseph*

"This guy can do it all. I hate him."
—*Satan*

"I was wrong. He is bigger than the Beatles."
—*John Lennon*

"Instead of scaring the hell out of the audience, he laughed the hell out of them."
—*Satan again*

JESUS DOES STAND-UP

Brian O'Connell

Copyright © 2024 J. Brian O'Connell
All Rights Reserved

 Year of the Book
135 Glen Avenue
Glen Rock, PA 17327

ISBN: 978-1-64649-447-7 (paperback)
ISBN: 978-1-64649-448-4 (ebook)

To purchase bulk copies, contact the publisher.

DEDICATION

This book is dedicated, first and foremost to My Lord and Savior, Jesus Christ, his dad, God, and the Holy Spirit, who guided me through this journey.

I must acknowledge everyone who has helped me with this peregrination, especially Raquel, who knows the Bible better than I ever will, and made me the man I am today; Colleen and Grant Williams, who make me look like a rookie in the parenting department; Cayden, who provided me with a piece of great advice for the book; Lincoln, the one family member who always makes me smile; Jim and Winnie, role models extraordinaire; Pastor Pete Ryder, your input and guidance proved invaluable and inspirational; Nick Elkevizth, without you, this book would not have a cover, thank you Jesus: Elena Valliere, without you, Jesus would not have a cover, you are always in my prayers; Nikki Brown, your insight and love of Jesus got me to the next level; Kevin O'Connell, Kathleen Williams, and Michael O'Connell, your lifelong encouragement has not gone unnoticed. Special thanks to PJ... I think of you every day.

Thank you to all of you.

Foreword

This book is not intended to offend anyone in any way. However, in this day and age, I am sure someone will reach out to regale me with why I'm going to rot in hell because of this book.

Throughout the history of comedy, comedians have used humor to make people more aware of certain topics. This publication was written with the intent of making people more aware of scripture. I don't intend for this book to be preachy. There are plenty of people around who can preach, and they are all much better than I am. However, if I can spark someone to pick up the Bible, even if it has been a long time since they read it, I'll consider it a win.

Jesus was a great communicator. When you look at the all-time great communicators, they all used comedy to some extent. While it may not be readily apparent in the Bible, I think Jesus must have had a humorous side. I don't think it is a stretch to imagine Jesus using stand-up comedy as a way of getting his message to the people.

I'm not making fun of the Bible. I'm finding humor in the Bible, there is a huge difference.

I invite you to come along with me as I attend a comedy show headlined by the very popular Jesus Christ.

IN THE GREEN ROOM

I'm following the owner of the club down a narrow hallway. He is leading me to the green room for an interview with Jesus and Jay Boc. As we enter the room, Jesus and Jay Boc are laughing. They immediately stand up to greet me. The owner tells us that he has prep work to do for the show and excuses himself. Jesus offers me a seat and we all sit down.

Me: **I've never been this nervous talking to anyone.**

Jesus: But you always talk to me. For the record, I've noticed that most of the time you are asking for something.

Me: **You keep track of that stuff?**

(Jesus nods his head. Jay stands up and excuses himself from the room.)

Me: **Well let's get to it. I'm really looking forward to the show tonight. Why stand-up and not a more traditional preaching role?**

Jesus: For years, stand-up comedy has been a medium to deliver a message in a nonthreatening way. People are more open to suggestion when they are laughing. If the "Book of Revelations" had predicted my return as a "Drybar Comedy Special," nobody would have taken it seriously. Besides, in Revelations I defeat Satan and his forces. In comedy, if you do well, they say you "killed it." So I'll be slaying the devil while killing the audience with laughter.

They say laughter is the best medicine. Coming together like this is healing. We are breaking down fences. Hebrews 10:24-25 and Ephesians 2:13 tell us how the far away are brought near. Not unlike cell phones and Zoom meetings today.

That being said, some people need to put the cell phones down for a minute. I know some audience members will be texting during the show... "I'm at a comedy show watching Jesus tell jokes...LOL."

Those people have no idea how overworked their guardian angels are because of cell phones. If my Real Dad wanted to cause a modern plague today all he would have to do is create a solar flare.

Me: **Why here? Why this venue?**

Jesus: What you don't know is that the idea of doing this show in Las Vegas was floated about. Somehow Sin City did not seem like a good fit. Instead of Jay Boc I would be working with Satan. Remember Luke 4? Satan spent 40 days trying to tempt me in the desert once before. He would have a field day in Vegas.

Can you imagine the Devil tempting me with show tickets, free buffets, and room upgrades if I would just give in to his requests? Nope, not doing that again!

Me: What type of comedy do you do? One-liners? Story format? Traditional?

Jesus: I use all forms. Some of my one-liners are more like dad jokes. For example:

Do you realize that Noah was the last human to see Bigfoot up close?

What was Noah's favorite fruit?
—*Pears! (Pairs).*

Noah was really old. He was about 600 years old when he was on the Ark. The Ark floated around for a year. You can't help but wonder if maybe Noah was just lost.

Seems like everyone in the Old Testament lived a *loooong* time... 800 or 900 years old was common. They were having kids at 100. Methuselah made it to 969! Kind of makes you wonder how old you had to be to get the senior discount at McDonald's.

Did you know that Noah had 3 sons? Ham, Japheth, and Shem. No one really liked Shem, they preferred Curly.
—*That is a weak 3-Stooges reference. You know it had to get boring on the Ark.*

What did they do for entertainment?
—*Jigsaw puzzles? It's impossible to find a jigsaw puzzle for ages 6 to 600.*

And you know it had to stink with all those animals. Have you ever been to a cat owner's home? I'm talking about the people with two or three cats, and they have not changed the litter box for a few days. Now just imagine the Ark with two of every animal for a year!

Hebrews 12:28 tells us that the Kingdom is unlike a James Bond martini.
—*It can't be shaken.*

Have any of you ever visited the Middle East? It really is a beautiful place. Do you know where Solomon's temple is?
—*It's on the side of his head.*

I recently rented a car to get around. They gave me my choice of any car on the lot...
—*So I picked out a Christler.*

Did you know that Purgatory was originally called Heck?

Are you familiar with Ananias from Acts? Specifically Acts 9:1-19.
—*Or as I like to refer to it, Better Call Saul.*

Me: **So, how much of your material comes from the Bible?**

Jesus: A lot of it does. I'm trying to take the familiar Bible stories and put a humorous spin on them. It doesn't take away from the message, it simply reinforces the message from another direction. Give me a Bible topic that most people would be familiar with, and I'll give you an example.

Me: **OK. How about your birth?**

Jesus: Good choice, especially since we are here in Bethlehem, Pennsylvania. This is a topic that can be approached from multiple angles.

When I was born, three Wise Men arrived from the east. I think they were from Persia. Matthew 2:1-2 references them arriving at a house bearing gifts. I'll get back to that in a minute.

Can you imagine if I was born in *this* Bethlehem? Instead of three Wise Men, I would have been visited by three *Wise Guys* from New Jersey.

Instead of gold, frankincense and myrrh, the Wise Guys would present gifts and say (with a New Jersey accent), "Here, we got dese for ya. We was walkin' down the road and dey fell off a truck."

Matthew writes that the Wise Men arrived at a house. If you recall, Herod wanted to do away with any male babies under two years old. By the time the Wise Men arrived we had left the stable. As I got older, Joseph and my mom would sometimes call after me when I ran out of the house and left the door open, "Were you born in a barn?" And I would say, "Yea, I sorta was."

Anyway, by the time the Wise Men arrived, I was about two years old. Parents with little ones in the house will back me up on this. When their kids were young, when they were toddlers, specifically in the Terrible Twos, patience was put to the test.

Now I want you to imagine the three Wise Men spending years, traveling thousands of miles only to meet a child going through his terrible twos. It might be hard to picture me hitting, kicking, biting, throwing things, while shouting, "NO, NO, NO." Trust me when I tell you this—and Joseph and my mom will back me up—there is no such thing as a Heavenly Temper Tantrum!

The Wise Men didn't stay long and I'm pretty confident that they left thinking, *THAT is the Messiah? Maybe we followed the wrong star, maybe we miscalculated Daniel 9:25.*

Me: **There is not much in the Bible about your youth. Do you shed more light on your life as a youngster?**

Jesus: Yes! Yes, I do. It's my way of reminding people that I was just like them in many ways.

If you think about it, Joseph was my step-dad. Step-parents have it hard. At some point the step-kids are going to hit you with, "I don't have to listen to you. You are not my real dad or real mom." It usually happens in the teen years.

There is a reason there is not much in the Bible about my teen years. There is also very little about Joseph. Most times we got along, but we had our moments. As a step-teen I wasn't always easy to get along with. Luke 2:41-52 mentions one incident. What you may not know is how things played out when we got home.

Joseph took me out to his workshop to have a talk with me. I reminded him that I had to go about my Real Dad's business. He explained to me that I was not yet ready to go off on my own and start preaching to the masses. He pointed out that I couldn't even keep my room clean.

He told me that at this point in my life I was not yet a Joel Osteen or David Jeremiah. He suggested that I learn a trade. Naturally he suggested carpentry. He opened his workshop doors and showed me a dining table and chairs he had made from a tree that he cut down. The craftsmanship was amazing. He told me that with time and patience that I too could learn to do that. He was such a kind soul.

Unfortunately for him, he was dealing with a know-it-all teen. I told him the table and chairs were very impressive, but my *Real* Dad had created the tree.

And that's why there isn't much in the Bible about my teen years. Joseph started spending more time with my siblings after that.

My mom would always compliment Joseph on his patience. Especially with my sisters. Parents with teen daughters can understand how nerves can be tested. If eye rolls made you dizzy, teenage girls would be staggering around like drunken sailors after exiting the Tilt-O-Whirl at an amusement park.

They say that God will test your strength and the Devil will test your weakness. Nobody warned you that teenagers will test your patience.

Whenever Joseph would get upset at us, he would quote Deuteronomy 32:35, "'Vengeance is mine,' sayeth the Lord." It's a good thing to keep in mind if you have kids.

It's also a good thing to remember when your neighbor starts cutting their grass at 7:00 AM on a Saturday morning. There is nothing more satisfying than putting things in God's hands, especially when the neighbor fires up his lawn mower at the crack of dawn.

Imagine that you are laying in bed when you suddenly hear the lawn mower, followed by a loud clap of thunder. You see lightning, and then the rain comes pouring down. It's amazing how soundly you will sleep after putting it in His hands. I can almost guarantee that the last thing you will hear before dozing off is your neighbor screaming, "But there was no rain in the forecast, where did those clouds come from?"

Sorry, I got off topic there.

Me: **You mentioned siblings. Tell me about your brothers and sisters.**

Jesus: Matthew 13:54-56 mentions my siblings. When you have siblings, you are better off being either the first or the baby. When you are a middle child you are always getting compared to the oldest. All you ever hear is, "Why can't you be more like your older brother or sister?"

Even if the oldest is a complete mess, you are still compared to them. "Thank goodness you are not like your older brother and/or sister." Parents compare you, teachers compare you, other kids compare you. For those of you who are middle kids, stop and think for a minute, what if your oldest brother was the Son of God! My sibs' only retort was to point out that I was only a step-brother. Kids can be so mean to each other.

It is written in scripture, "Go forth and multiply." But it is also written, "In this world you will have trouble." It seems to me, all that multiplying has contributed to the trouble.

Me: We don't know much about your youth. What did you enjoy doing as a kid?

Jesus: It was a typical Jewish upbringing. I had chores and responsibilities. We observed all of the Jewish holidays and traditions. As a young boy I would have sleepovers with my friends. Our favorite activity was sitting around a campfire and telling scary stories.

I always went last because I had the scariest stories. I got most of my material from the Old Testament. The OT is not for the faint of heart. There is stuff in there that you could not show on TV during the family-hour. The OT has flaming swords, murder, giants, snakes... and that's just Genesis. The book, not the Phil Collins and Peter Gabriel group.

Me: Was a sense of humor common in your household?

Jesus: I grew up in a household that had a sense of humor. Remember when I was hanging around at the Mount of Olives? It's a beautiful place and I was just meditating and reflecting. If you know John 8:1-9, you know what's coming. The teachers of the law and the Pharisees brought me a woman and accused her of adultery. The Law of Moses commanded stoning for such an infraction, and I'm not talking about the good type of stoning... ahem, the stoning that involves plant life.

Anyway, I called out, "Let any one of you who is without sin be the first to throw a stone at her." Eventually the crowd dispersed leaving me and the woman.

Suddenly out of nowhere a stone comes flying toward us. It caught both of us off guard. Startled, I turned to see a figure approaching us. It took me a moment, but I recognized the stone tosser. I called out, "Mom! I'm trying to work here!" Fortunately, my mom had a pretty good arm so she was confident that she would not hit us with the rock.

Me: **What is God like?**

Jesus: That's the million-dollar question. He's really complex. The Bible says that God is the same yesterday, today, and forever. But I'm here to tell you that my *real dad* changed somewhat as time passed. I would like to interject that Hollywood sort of got God right. He really is a cross between George Burns and Morgan Freeman.

The best way to describe God is for you to think of your own parents. The people who raised you had all kinds of rules for you to follow. They made you earn everything they gave you. You probably had curfews to abide by, certain friends you were not allowed to hang out with, and multiple chores. When those same people became grandparents, their mindset changed.

Dads had RULES! Granddads were more like, "What are these RULES you speak of?" The same people who would not let you have dessert or go out to play unless you ate all of your dinner are giving their grandkids candy for dinner and ice cream for dessert. They are different people than the ones who raised you. Grandparents are more like the New Testament God.

I think it's fair to say that my *real dad* had a bit of a temper in the Old Testament. He sent floods, plagues, and tested your loyalty to him.

He was the Original Gangster. You might say he was the OG of the OT.

If you read John 17, you get to see him through my eyes, you can understand his love and gain a sense that he seems to have mellowed out in the New Testament.

Me: **Free will seems like a subject that has some comedy fodder. Any thoughts?**

Jesus: Ahh, free will. If you are familiar with 1 Corinthians 10:13 then you know something about free will. Free will can be confusing. If you are a guy in a relationship, you already understand how confusing free will can be. When a woman says, "Go ahead, do what you want," what she is actually saying is, "*Don't* do what *you* want!" God's free will is his way of saying, do what you want, but there are consequences for your actions.

Guys have learned that the phrase, "whatever, do what you want" is not really a choice. There will be consequences. Before you do what *you* want with your free will, a smart man would reassess how comfortable the couch is.

Free will can cause a phobia called Decidophobia, which most often affects men after a certain number of years of marriage. It's the fear of making decisions. For the married guys it's not so much the fear, it's that they just forgot how to make a decision. Ultimately, they got tired of being wrong.

This may go back to the Garden of Eden. I'm not saying this is exactly how it happened, but to be fair, it is possible that Eve was experimenting with some of the other plants before she got the munchies and grabbed the apple. Let's examine *her* story. The Devil, posing as a snake convinces her to take a bite of the apple. The *snake* tells her to eat the apple. Eve claims that a *talking* snake told her to eat the apple. A *talking snake*. It's not like Eve's last name was Doolittle!

Adam shows up to find Eve and immediately realizes that she is paranoid, a side effect from the happy-weed. Eve tells Adam he has to take a bite from the apple too. Mostly because my Real Dad had not created chips and munchies yet. Anyway, after they both eat from the apple, they realize they are naked. As the happy-weed is starting to wear off, they become aware of their nakedness. They never noticed they were naked while they were high.

God shows up in the garden and the first thing Adam does is blame Eve. Then, and this is the good part, he sort of blames God by saying, "The woman *you* put here with me gave me the fruit." And that is why married couples argue till this day.

I want to point out one more thing about this interaction. Notice how Eve got Adam to eat the fruit. She said, "Here, eat this."

And he said okey dokey. Guys don't offer to share food like women do. When a guy wants a woman to eat some of his food, he usually prefaces it with something like, "Here try this. Does it taste funny to you?"

Me: **How do you tie the Bible to modern times using humor?**

Jesus: I use many of the same tools that other stand-up comics use. I take advantage of the use of premises, set-ups, and punchlines. I have stories, one-liners, and quick hitters, and I'll tie multiple topics together.

For example, I may ask the audience if any of them are list makers. They know who they are. I'm talking about people who make lists for everything. These same people will list item #1, "Make a list." They do that just so that they immediately have something to check off.

The most famous list maker in the OT was a guy named Moses. Maybe you've heard of him. According to Exodus he spent 40 days on the mountain getting the 10 commandments. The truth is he just wanted to get away from everyone. He kept hearing complaints about being lost, being hungry, being thirsty, being pursued by armies, blah blah blah. We will talk more about that later. I can now tell you that Moses was just killing time, trying to get away from everyone.

But here is the breaking news... My Real Dad gave Moses 1 commandment. That's right. Just ONE COMMANDMENT—"Be Good!" Pretty simple, huh? Moses made up the other 9 so he could justify being away from everyone for 40 days.

You may be familiar with Exodus and the story of Moses leading people out of slavery. These were the same group of complainers I just talked about. They thought they were lost, they got hungry, thirsty, and angry. They were the first people identified as Hangry!

Some of you may live with someone who has that gene. They would ask Moses, in a sarcastic tone, "What's the deal here? Didn't Egypt have any graves, so you brought us to the desert to die?"

Hangry and Sarcasm are a bad duo. Worse than Sean Penn and Madonna. Not my mom, the other Madonna.

See how I'm tying multiple topics together here?

Anyway, when Moses parted the Red Sea and everyone scampered through, some of the people picked up some sea creatures as they made their way to safety. We know this because Exodus 26:14 mentions tents made with Dugongs. Dugong skin is a sea creature hide. These people were in the desert! Where are they getting sea creature hides? I'm pretty sure that they didn't stop at Dugongs-R-Us. It's a way of reminding us that when things look bleak my Real Dad comes through.

Looking at the night sky through your tent made of Dugong hides should cause you to think about the good in your life and be thankful. So I encourage you to greet others with, "Tell me about your Dugong!"

Before we get too far away from Exodus, I want to clarify 3:14. It says, "I am who I am." It has absolutely nothing to do with Popeye. It is *not*, I yam who I yam.

Hopefully that gives a little insight into how I take a simple topic like list making and tie it into Moses, Exodus, Dugong, and a Popeye reference.

Me: **Do you talk about ministers, preachers and priests in your show?**

Jesus: Ahh, The Pulpit Masters! I could do a whole show about men, and women, of the cloth. Like any profession, the make-up of personalities is all inclusive. Let me be the first to say, none of them have *all* of the answers. Not while they are on this side of the dirt anyway. Some are divine-like, and some end up being more divisive than divine. Sometimes they seem more focused on making sure you don't raise hell when maybe they should be getting the congregation to raise a hallelujah.

I'm sure we will have a lot of clergy and religious people in the audience tonight. I will give a shout out and thank them for all their years of support and faith. I know some of them are anticipating an evening of parables and preaching. But that is not what tonight is all about. At least not overtly.

(Jesus winked at me and smiled as he said that. I can't begin to describe how comforting a wink and a smile from Jesus is. It's like having your favorite relative wink at you at the dinner table after he tells an inside joke. It's a special acknowledgment. It's a welcoming gesture that makes you feel special).

Jesus: I'll probably tell this story on stage tonight, and it may be the closest I get to a parable, but I'll let you in on it now.

It's about Father Al Frankel. Father Al is an unassuming man and incredibly humble. One evening he was in his bedroom opening his mail. One of the letters was from home. In addition to a nice note, the letter included a $100 bill. Not the kind of bill you pay, the kind you spend. As Father Al sat back thinking about how he would spend the gift, he glanced out of his window and saw a man leaning against a street lamp. The man had his hat pulled down and his coat collar turned up. His hands were tucked deep in his pockets trying to keep warm.

Father Al kept glancing back and forth at the man on the street and his brand new fortune. After several minutes of deep thought and prayer, he grabbed a pencil and pad from his desk and wrote a simple note. It said, "Don't Despair!" He then wrapped the 100-dollar bill and the note around the pencil and secured them with a rubber band. Next, he opened the window and tossed the pencil toward the man leaning on the lamp post.

The stranger picked up the pencil, slowly read the note, and lifted the brim of his hat as he looked up to Father Al's window. He gave Father Al a thumbs up sign and dashed off down the street.

The next night as Father Al was reading Luke 3:11 there was a knock at the door. It was the stranger from the night before. He handed Father Al an envelope and walked away without saying a word. Upon opening the envelope Father Al found $6,000 in it. Six thousand dollars! Father Al called out to the man, "I don't understand!"

Without turning around, the man called back, "Don't Despair paid 60 to 1."

(Then, keeping with the preaching theme he initiated, Jesus continued the conversation.)

Jesus: Some people were a little concerned when they learned I was going to be performing stand-up comedy. They thought I should stick to the tried-and-true P&P format. For those who don't know, P&P is Preaching & Parables.

(In his best Groucho Marx voice)

> Not to be confused with the old A&P for the people of a certain vintage in the crowd.
>
> I share with people that laughter is mentioned numerous times in the Bible. One of my favorites is Psalm 126. Since we are talking about Psalms, who came up with the spelling of Psalm? You know that word

has knocked an untold number of kids out of spelling bees. Sure, it looks good on paper if you combine it with the P&P for the Preaching & Parables. PP&P. Preaching, Parables & Psalms. But it doesn't exactly roll off the tongue when you say it.

(*He says it with emphasis on the first letter.* "P"reaching "P"arables and *p*"S"alms.)

Jesus: Speaking of parables, are you familiar with Luke 15:11-32? Most people know it as the story about the prodigal son. Or the lost son. It follows the lost sheep parable and the lost coin parable. Apparently, people kept losing things back then. Today the parables would be about lost keys, lost cell phones, lost passwords, and lost minds.

Here's the *Readers Digest* version. Do you think I need to tell the younger audience members that *Readers Digest* was a periodical with short stories and silly jokes?

Anyway, we have a father with two sons. The youngest decides he wants his half of the inheritance now. He doesn't want to wait. He takes the money and blows it all in a far-off land, presumably Los Angeles or New York. After he loses all his money and falls on hard times, he decides to go back home and ask for forgiveness, and a place to live.

Back in the olden days—the 1950s, 60s, and 70s—once a child left the home, they would only come back to visit. I know this seems like science fiction to some people, but kids actually moved out, and stayed out. But once again I digress.

Anyway, his father is so happy to see him that he throws a party. This really upsets the other brother who has stayed behind to help around the house and tend to the property. The brother that stayed at home proclaims, "That ain't fair!" To which his father replies—

Me: **"Life ain't fair!"**

(Jesus smiles.)

Jesus: Amen, brother.

(Impersonating Paul Harvey...)

"And now for the rest of the story."

(Jesus actually does pretty good impersonations...)

It wasn't the father who decided to welcome his son back with a party. In fact, he was happy to see him, but he didn't want to throw a party. It was the mom! Even back then the women were in charge.

When you realize the Bible is written by men, you can start to understand why women get so little credit. The mom wanted a party because she found her lost son. Just like women find everything today. How often does a man ask his wife, "Where is my wallet?" And she'll say, "On the dresser where you left it."

"Where are my lost sheep?"
—*"In the pasture near the creek."*

Men don't even try to look any more. They just ask the woman in their life. If it wasn't for women, men would get lost trying to find heaven.

I'm reminded of the story about a man who joined a monastery. The monks could only speak two words per year. A young man is called in after Year 1 for his evaluation. He is given permission to speak:

Head Monk: You have permission to say two words.

Young Monk: Bed, hard.

Year 2

Head Monk: You have been here two years. You have permission to say two words.

Young Monk: Food, terrible.

Year 3

Head Monk: You have been here three years. You have permission to say two words.

Young Monk: I QUIT!

Head Monk: Good riddance! All you've done for three years is complain!

Me: **Would we be surprised to learn who is in Heaven and who isn't?**

Jesus: You may be surprised!

Do you remember a group called the Beatles? For the under-40 crowd, at one time they were a pretty popular band. One of the members was a guy named John Lennon. In an interview in 1966, Lennon was quoted as saying, "We're more popular than Jesus now." Needless to say, that comment caught the attention of several high-ranking folks on the other side of the Pearly Gates.

Let's fast forward to December 8, 1980. Saint Peter was manning the Pearly Gates. He looked at his list of new arrivals, and greeted John with "Mr. Lennon, God wanted to see you as soon as you arrived." Saint Peter picked up the phone and simply said, "He's here!" A split-second later Lennon was standing in front of God.

A minute after that, I showed up with popcorn. By the time I got settled in, my Real Dad was holding a newspaper clipping. He proceeded to question Lennon, "Did you really think that you were more popular than my son?"

Lennon looked down and started shuffling his feet like a six year old who got caught stealing cookies. He stammered, "We were a pretty big thing back then!"

To which my Real Dad replied, "Oh I know, but bigger than Christianity?"

Seeing how nervous Lennon was, God told him that all was forgiven. And to show that there were no hard feelings he revealed that Lennon would spend eternity looking like he did in the 1960s. Lennon thanked God and left for his heavenly orientation.

Afterward, I asked God why He let him off the hook so easy. He replied, "John suffered enough on earth. Remember, I put Yoko in his life."

If this was a modern-day parable, the lesson might be that you need to appreciate your spouse. Your spouse may just be your personal ONO. Think of them as your YOKO PASS into Heaven.

Me: Who else?

Jesus: Do you know who Madalyn Murray O'Hair is?

Me: No, who is she?

Jesus: She is the woman responsible for removing prayer from public schools in 1963. She may be the most famous atheist of her time. I don't call her an atheist. I refer to her as a GODOPHOBE.

Me: A what?

Jesus: A GODOPHOBE. Someone who doesn't believe in God or is afraid of God. I can see how someone might be afraid of God if all you ever read was the Old Testament. He was pretty intimidating, but if you read the New Testament, I think you'll have a more well-rounded picture of my Real Dad. He really is a loving God.

Some phobias make sense to me. Take Arachibutyrophobia, which is the fear of having peanut butter stuck to the roof of your mouth. I thought that only dogs had that fear. In the world of phobias, GODOPHOBEs are a group that can probably be reduced with very little effort.

There I go again, getting off topic. Anyway, Madalyn Murray O'Hair got to visit Heaven on a 1-day pass. We wanted to show her what she was missing. Her only response was "OOPS."

Did you know Cleopatra is in Heaven? She and St. Patrick have the most interesting discussions about snakes.

Me: **Are all of the Apostles in Heaven?**

Jesus: Absoheavenlylutly! That's a word that will win you lots of Scrabble games.

They are my friends. To put it in street terms, if you have my back, I'll have yours.

Me: **What can you tell me about them that may not be common knowledge?**

Jesus: Let's talk about some of my closest friends. I've always thought that a good sobriety test would be to have the person name all 12 Apostles. Forget walking a straight line or saying the alphabet backwards. Imagine the police officer walks up to your car. The cop says, "Do you know why I pulled you over? Have you been drinking or are you on any medications? I'll need you to step out of the car. Are you a Christian?" At this point the driver is saying, "Yes. Wait. What, why?"

The policeman advises that he thinks the driver is impaired. Then he says, "I'll need you to name the 12 Apostles."

Feeling confident the driver starts: "Peter, Simon... No, wait. I think they were both the same guy. Judas, Jude... was he the same guy as Judas? Matthew, Mark, Luke, and John, how many is that? 6? Let's make Peter and Simon two different people then. Same with Judas and Jude. That gives me 8, right? Wasn't there a tax guy? I don't know his name but I should get credit for him. I'm up to 9, right? James! There was a James, right? Two more to go. Hmmm, Cherubim and Seraphim. Now it's your turn, can you name the 10 Commandments? Go ahead, name them and I'll let you go!"

Policeman: "Sir, I pulled *you* over."

Driver: "You didn't name the 10 Commandments, and some of my Apostles may be incorrect, so let's just call it even, and go our own way."

Policeman: "OK, Father. See you Sunday."

For the record, the driver would be incorrect. My friends were Simon Peter, Thomas, Judas, Andrew, Bartholomew, James the brother of John, James the lesser, John, Thaddeus, Matthew, Philip, Simon, and I'll give you Matthias since he replaced Judas, he was our "player to be named later" in the line-up.

My friends were of varying professions. Many were fishermen, one was a tax collector, one was royalty, one was a zealot, and several were writers, but you know who wasn't in the group?

Lawyers and politicians! I would have accepted them, but they didn't want anything to do with me. I assume it's because we didn't have much money. Plus, they would have had to give up *everything* and follow me. I don't see that happening. Lawyers and politicians complain when they have to give up a private parking space.

Let's start with Peter. He could be a little hot headed. Luke 22:49-51 tells us about the time that Peter cut off the ear of one of the men who came to arrest me. The poor guy was a servant of one of the high priests. What you might not know is that the servant's last name was Van Gogh.

Many people already know that Judas betrayed me, and we will talk more about him in a minute. But before that I need to tell you about the first guy to betray me.

Immediately after Peter separated the servant from his ear, another follower undermined me. As I was reattaching the ear, a little-known follower named Legalese jumped into action. Legalese handed the servant his personal injury business card. It said, "Legalese Lawyerous, personal injury lawyer. If you or a loved one has suffered a personal injury, we can help. Specializing in chariot accidents, boating mishaps, stonings, and rogue goat stampedes."

Now you know why none of the Apostles were lawyers.

Getting back to Judas. He really was one of my favorites. If you look at the big picture, he was just doing what he was destined to do. Sure, he was a thief per John 12, but I trusted him. He held the purse strings. He would complain sometimes. He hated it when my feet were washed with perfume. That's why I never mentioned the shampoo and conditioner that I picked up on my visits into town. To this day, I truly believe that some of my followers were simply fans of my long hair. I was Fabio, before Fabio.

This is a good opportunity to put the Last Supper into perspective. First of all, it almost didn't happen. When we showed up at the room, it was reserved by a local Fraternal Group—Oddfellows, Moose, Elks, Rotary, I don't recall who (but I know it wasn't the Knights of Columbus because Columbus was 1400 years from being born)—had the room reserved. We got them to switch venues by agreeing to buy tickets to their reverse raffle.

We all have some family members and friends who will fight over the check when we go out to eat. It seems like the same people are always fighting for the check while that one relative or friend has the T-Rex arms. It was no different with the Apostles.

Before we knew it, we started hearing, "All I ordered was water; who ordered appetizers? We have 6 orders of matza ball soup on the check; did everybody have wine? Who got dessert? Let's just split it 13 ways; Matthew has a coupon; why does Thomas always go use the bathroom when the check comes?"

To settle matters, I told Judas to pick up the check and leave a 20 percent tip. Judas was not happy about paying the bill and when I mentioned the tip, he reminded me that

Hebrews 7:1-2 only mentions 10 percent. To which I replied...

"Hey Jude, don't let me down.
You have found her, now go and get her."

He had no way of knowing that those lyrics would be part of a Lennon-McCartney tune on Apple records 2000 years later. There's that apple again.

My friend Thomas was also known as "Doubting Thomas." It's an unfortunate nickname. First of all, "Doubting Didymus" has a much better ring to it. It's all spelled out in John 20:24-29.

In fact, we learn a lot in John 20. Did you know that the Apostles competed in the early Olympics? Mary was the fastest, followed by John and Peter. When I rose from the dead, Mary ran so fast she got dizzy and didn't even recognize me. Peter can run too but nobody can run like John. What you may not know is that while John can outrun Peter, Peter was a much stronger swimmer. For years they bickered about who would have gotten to my tomb first, if my tomb was on an island. I never had the heart to tell them that a disciple named Gilligan probably would have been the first to arrive if the tomb was on an island.

If I had assigned nicknames, John was so fast, he would be called "Johnny Wheels the Beloved."

Getting back to Thomas. He was not there when I arose from the dead and appeared to the other Apostles. I think they sent him out for Chinese food. Anyway, about a week after Thomas said he would not be a believer unless he put his hand in my wounds, I appeared in front of Thomas. It's hard to capture the magnitude of the moment, but let's just say it was one of my greatest "Hold My Beer" moments ever.

So, let's get back to hypothetical nicknames. Per Mark 14:66-68, in a scripture familiar to most of us, Peter should probably be called "Peter the Fibber."

Here's a tidbit you may not know. In Mark 14:51-52, the naked guy is Mark himself. Leaving me no choice but to nickname him "The Streak!"

Some people know that one of my favorite disciples was Mary Magdalene. I'm sure you're wondering where I'm going with this. Well, the truth is, Mary and I had some deep discussions, and our share of disagreements. It wasn't always like Acts 2. We didn't always understand each other.

Sometimes it was more like Genesis 11. Just to reiterate, I mean the book and not the band. Back then the descendants of Noah lived in the area of Mesopotamia (not to be confused with Mesothelioma), in Babylon. The Babylonians, led by a guy named Nimrod, wanted to build a giant tower all the way to the heavens to protect themselves in case God ever decided to flood the earth again.

GOD, My Real Dad did not appreciate their arrogance, so he suddenly had everyone speaking different languages. Nimrod could not complete his tower.

My point is, when you are close to someone, sometimes you just can't communicate as well as you would like. It's not uncommon for people to have enthusiastic discussions with people close to them. Maybe they argue about who was going to fill up the car, or who was supposed to buy the tickets, or who was going to make reservations.

It's amazing how often these discussions end with someone being called a "Nimrod."

Me: **What bugs you?**

Jesus: I ask you to keep in mind my practical joker side when *you* are praying, or should I say, *negotiating* with me or God. I can't begin to count how many times we've heard, "If you can just do this, I promise to do that." Some of you sound like defense attorneys.

"Dear God, help me pass this test and I promise to study every night."

"Dear God, just get me out of this situation and I'll go to church every week."

"Dear Jesus, take the wheel..." Just so you know, I'm not literally going to drive for you. Keep your mitts on the steering wheel!

Or one of my favorites: A man is on a diet. The Devil tempts him with a craving for a donut. The man prays, Dear Jesus, I'll be driving by the donut shop in five minutes. I'll only stop if there is a parking spot right in front of the door. That man drove around the block seven times before a spot opened up at the front door!

You can put your faith in me and let me handle it. I repeat, let *me* handle it. Have you ever been asked to do a project by someone because they didn't know how to do it? Then they proceed to tell you how to do it. Don't be *that* person when you ask me to do something for you. Leave it in my hands, and don't try to negotiate.

Me: **What are some of your favorite Bible stories?**

Jesus: That's a tough one. There are so many. Have you ever read the book of Judges in the Bible? It reads like a modern-day true crime series. A woman kills a guy named Sisera by driving a tent pole through his temple. Trust me when I tell you that this is not a collection of case rulings by Judge Wapner or Milan on *People's Court*.

There is one story that still has me scratching my head. There are some things in the Bible that are just flat out strange. In 2 Kings 2:23-25, a traveler, Elisha, encounters some children who mocked him and teased him for being bald.

The traveler cursed the kids, and out of nowhere a couple of bears appeared and destroyed the kids. I know what you are thinking... *I don't remember hearing about that in Bible school*. That's because this is a terrifying story to tell little kids. It would scare the crap out of them.

Imagine kids hearing this and then walking home from church or Bible school. Picture them as they walk past the house of the grumpy old *bald* man in the neighborhood, the same guy who always yells at them to get off of his lawn.

Now imagine that at this very moment someone rides by with a large growling dog. *Grrrr!* These kids would not even look around. They would all start running because their little minds would be imagining a bear is coming to eat them.

To make matters worse, these kids would be traumatized every time their mom told them to get the bottle of Mr. Clean from under the sink. Parents everywhere would be tucking kids in at night by telling them that there are no bald men monsters under the bed, and no bald men with bears under the kitchen sink.

The only way this story makes any sense is if it is situated in Wisconsin, the kids are Green Bay Packer fans, and the old man is a bald Mike Ditka.

As a side note, Elisha went on to become the founder of the Hair Club for Men.

One of my favorite stories sometimes has its characters mixed up with an animated movie, especially when children try to retell it. That happens to me sometimes too. Especially with Numbers 22.

It's a story about a man named Balaam who has a conversation with his donkey, a talking donkey. I'm not ruling out that Balaam had gotten ahold of Eve's wacky tobacky. The talking donkey got me to think about the movie *Shrek*. In that context, you can't help but imagine the talking donkey sounding just like Eddie Murphy. So naturally, Shrek, er I mean Balaam, has to sound like Mike Myers.

Let me give you a little background. Balaam and his donkey are traveling down a narrow road. An angel appears, but only the donkey can see and hear the angel. So the donkey veers off the main road onto a narrower path. The angel appears again. Again, the donkey sees him, but Balaam does not. The donkey detours once more and Balaam begins to beat the donkey. This is where Balaam starts talking to the donkey, and we learn that the donkey can talk back.

So here is the exchange between Balaam and the donkey in the voices of Myers and Murphy.

Donkey/Murphy: "What have I done to make you beat me?"

Balaam/Shrek/Myers: "You made a fool of me."

At this point, Balaam's eyes were opened and he finally saw an angel with a sword.

The angel says (in the voice of Cameron Diaz): "The donkey saw me and turned away three times. If he had not turned away, I would have had to kill you!"

Now I don't know what kind of comment the Eddie Murphy donkey would make in that situation, but I'm guessing it would have something to do with Balaam being saved by a smart ass. In my opinion, Balaam should have kissed his ass.

I have a history of casting out demons. But I'm also a bit of a practical joker. An example of this can be found in Luke 8:26-33. I arrived in the Gerasenes region and a man possessed by demons comes to greet me. I learned that he was possessed by many demons. The demons begged me not to cast them into the bottomless pit. The demons asked that instead I cast them into some nearby pigs. I granted their request. The demons were cast into the herd of pigs, and not into the bottomless pit.

Immediately after the transfer, the entire herd of pigs were plunged down a steep hillside, into the lake where they drowned. As the demons were drowning, I could hear them singing, "My bologna has a first name, It's O-S-C-A-R..."

I'll let you in on a little secret about me. This will make more sense to you if you are familiar with Mark 11:12-21. Anyway, I can get *hangry* sometimes. I once cursed a fig tree because I was hungry. The tree ended up shriveling and dying. For most of you, when you are hangry it translates into just being grumpy. It is a little more serious in my case. Do you really think it is a coincidence that so many Bible stories involve food? Being hangry is the Devil's blessing, not God's.

Me: **Does your show have a message?**

Jesus: *(Laughing)* Of course it does. Everything I do has a message. My shows are all about love. Love and laughter go together. People love babies. Everybody I know smiles and/or laughs when a baby smiles or laughs. Babies are so full of love that they can make people smile even if the baby is angry or upset. By making people laugh, I'm spreading love. I'm asking them to embrace their inner child and laugh freely.

When the audience embraces love, the club becomes a church. Laughter begets love, love begets the church. I urge you to check out Acts 2:46-47. "Every day they devoted themselves to meeting together in the temple, and broke bread from house to house. They ate their food with *joyful* and sincere hearts, praising God and enjoying the favor of all the people. Every day the Lord added to their number those who were being saved."

So I guess what I'm saying is... by going to *this* comedy show on the weekend you can skip getting up early on Sunday. Just as I have come to serve, don't forget to tip your server. Contrary to what some believe, tipping is not the same as tithing.

If you look to find the humor in your daily life, love will not be far behind. Let me share with you what love is in the minds of children. Love is:

"When my grandmother got arthritis, she could not bend over and paint her toenails anymore... So my grandfather does it for her all of the time, even when his hands have arthritis too. That's love." —Rebecca, age 8

"Love is what makes you smile even when you are tired." —Colleen, age 4

"Love is what's in the room with you at Christmas if you stop opening presents and just listen." —Cayden, age 7

And one more. Lincoln is a 4-year-old whose next door neighbor was an elderly gentleman who recently lost his wife. Upon seeing the man cry, Lincoln went into the elderly gentleman's yard, climbed into the porch swing, and just quietly sat next to the man. When his mother asked what he had said to the neighbor, Lincoln replied, "Nothing, I just helped him cry."

Speaking of churches, I've always been fascinated by the exercise churches. Let me be clear, I'm not talking about exorcisms! I'm referencing the churches where the services have you constantly moving. The whole thing is a combination of standing, sitting, kneeling, and so forth. It's a professionally choreographed routine. I call it Prayer Aerobics.

Imagine Richard Simmons leading the service in his red and white striped shorts.

(Jesus begins to act out while he is talking.)

And a one, and a two, and the Father and the Son, and the Holy Spirit, and kneel, and sit, and kneel, and stand… The Father and the

Son and the Holy Spirit, and sit, and stand, and kneel, and stand… Can you feel the burn? Better to feel it here than in the afterlife. And kneel, and stand, and kneel, and stand… Reach high now. And the Father, and the Son, and the Holy Spirit…

(Suddenly there is a knock on the door followed by an anonymous voice…)

"Five minutes, JC."

Showtime

The excitement in the club is through the roof. People have waited in line for hours, and now that they are in the room and seated, they are giddy. The waitstaff and bartenders are swamped with food and drink orders. The full house has the staff cheerfully attending to everyone's needs.

I'm seated in the center of the room, seven rows back. It's the perfect spot to watch the show and feel the audience vibe.

The lights go down and a God-like voice bellows out an announcement about club etiquette: "Please keep your talking to a minimum but laughter to a maximum. Do not record the comedians." The authoritative voice covers the food and drink specials and introduces the master of ceremonies (MC) for the evening. I know this show is going to be special when the MC turns out to be the club owner.

The MC tells a couple of jokes, mentions some of the upcoming acts in the weeks ahead and introduces the opening act. The opening act is a comedian named Jay Boc. Jay has a reputation as a clean comic. In many clubs he would be the headliner, but not tonight, not when Jesus is in the line-up. Jay performs for about 30 minutes and the crowd really seems to enjoy his set.

When Jay wraps up, the MC comes back on stage to introduce the main act. "Tonight's headliner does not need an introduction. Ladies and gentlemen, I have the great honor and pleasure to present our headliner for the evening. You've read about him in the Bible, some call him the Star of the New Testament. He's here by way of the Middle East. Put your hands together for our Shepherd, our Savior, the one and only Son of God, the almighty Jesus Christ."

The room goes wild. There is wall-to-wall applause and cheers, a woman faints. Jesus walks on stage and immediately approaches the lady who fainted. She is a little groggy but fully recovers as soon as she touches the robe of Jesus.

The star is followed by the spotlight. At first glance I thought the spotlight was following him, but after closer observation, I come to realize, He *IS* the Light.

In spite of his simple attire, he looks absolutely majestic. Jesus waves and smiles to the crowd. He is confident, his smile is warm and comforting.

(As the noise dies down Jesus speaks...)

Jesus: Thank you, thank you. It's nice to be here. It's so nice seeing so many familiar faces. My good friend Lazarus is here. Good to see you again, you are looking healthy. The last time I saw you, you looked, shall we say, a little under the weather.

(The crowd roars with laughter.)

Barabbas is here too. He was reluctant at first. The last time we were both in the same venue it didn't work out so well for me. He really didn't want to attend tonight, but I reminded him that he sort of owed me one."

(All of the women looked around and clutched their purses a little tighter.)

I probably should *not* have pointed him out, but you can relax. I have it on good authority that he is no longer a thief. He is reformed.

It's great to be here for the first stop of my tour. My tour manager is Paul. Some of you know that it is estimated that Paul traveled over 10,000 miles, on foot! That's almost equivalent to walking across the U.S. four times. Naturally anyone who logs that much time visiting places knows the best spots to eat and stay, and would naturally be an obvious choice to be my agent and tour manager.

I have to tell you that I was very excited when my booking agent, Paul, told me I would be performing in Bethlehem. My first thought was, I will be kicking things off at the place where it all began. What he neglected to tell me was... it is Bethlehem, *Pennsylvania!*

Some have asked me why I decided to do comedy. There are really three reasons. First, comedy is an effective way to get a message across to people. Second, laughter and joy are mentioned more than 200 times in the Bible, and finally, according to some guests at Cana...

I CAN'T DANCE VERY WELL.

(Just then the sound system starts blasting "Jesus is Just Alright," by the Doobie Brothers, and Jesus starts dancing all over the stage. Some of the crowd stands up and dances at their seats. After 2-3 minutes the music dies down and cheers erupt from the room.)

Jesus: Bet you weren't expecting *that*, were you? For all of these years you thought I was invited to weddings because of the wine and water thing. Now you know, it was because *I can dance!*

Let me tell you something that didn't make it into the Bible. The Apostles and I actually did the Electric Slide at the Last Supper. They had no idea what electricity was. The room was lit with oil lamps. The "Oil Lamp Slide" doesn't exactly roll off of the tongue, so the name of the dance didn't really catch on until 2000 years later.

I want to give a shout out to the management of this club for putting me up at a really nice place. You may have heard of it. It's called the "No Room at the Inn" Inn.

It's a hotel with theme rooms. They have several rooms. One of my favorites is the "Herod room." Kids under two years old are not permitted. If you didn't get that, check out Matthew 2:16-18.

I'm staying in the "Stable room." It has a full-size manger, and animal sounds play all night in Dolby surround sound. The hotel goes the extra mile to make it feel authentic. They keep pumping in barn animal smells. It's their version of aroma therapy.

Sleeping at night can be a challenge because a really bright light keeps shining in through the window. I don't know if it's a star or a street light. The absolute biggest drawback, the worst part of this particular room, is that uninvited strangers keep popping in at all hours, specifically, shepherds and Maji.

Oh, before I forget, management here at the Bethlehem Comedy Club asked me to mention tonight's dinner specials. You can choose between the Exodus 16—which includes Manna and quail—or the Mark 6, which has 5 loaves and 2 fishes. We also are serving a Noah pizza. The

Noah pizza is a meat lovers pizza, but because it's a Noah pizza we do not include the ham.

Working in the kitchen tonight is the world-famous chef, Lot. You may remember him from the trendy, some would say decadent, restaurant Sodom & Gomorrah. Naturally, every meal is prepared as a low-salt dish.

We were going to use him to valet the cars, but we already had a parking Lot. See what I did there?

Our drink special tonight is Cana wine. Just a heads up… don't order water expecting me to do something about it. I am not doing *that* tonight.

(Jesus spots a lady eating fish with red wine. He immediately covers her plate and glass with a large napkin. When he removes the cover, the fish is a pot roast.)

I told you that I wasn't going to do the wine thing.

This club is also serving a Blushing Angel. It's one and a half ounces of red Dubonnet, one splash of cranberry juice, five ounces of chilled sparkling wine, and a lemon twist. It probably goes without saying, but all of the cocktails are made with *Holy* Spirits.

(We are only a few minutes into his set and his charisma is overwhelming. It makes me wonder why the gospels didn't do more to highlight Jesus' sense of humor. He knows how to read a room and get his message across. The fact that he has comedic timing is an unexpected bonus.

As the set progresses, he covers much of the same material that he referenced during our interview in the green room. Many of those jokes and stories are fine-tuned and succinct. He deftly sprinkles in one-liners, stories, and observations without missing a beat. His approach is so conversational that the audience doesn't even recognize the set-up for the joke until the punchline is delivered. An example of this plays out when he starts talking about Bible beaters.)

> Jay Boc was telling me before the show that his parents taught him a lot about the Bible. Whenever he acted up, his parents would hit him with the Bible. They were literally, old-fashioned Bible beaters.

(His next move shows how great he is at incorporating audience participation, with a joke callback. It's easy to see why he has so many followers. He grabs your attention with a simple, unexpected statement.)

> I've always been a fan of game shows. Some of my favorites were "Who Do You Trust" and "Let's Make a Deal." I can't begin to count how many

times people want to Make-A-Deal when times are tough.

Naturally, I enjoyed "To Tell the Truth" and of course "Truth or Consequences" for obvious reasons. Tonight, we are going to play our own little game show. The name of the show is "Location or Medication?"

The winners will receive a t-shirt that says, "Tell me about your Dugong."

(Who would have expected a call-back in a bit about game shows?)

I'll give you a name and you tell me if it is a medication or a location in the Bible. I'll give you fair warning, we are not picking places like Jerusalem, Capernaum, or Bethlehem. Raise your hand if you want to play.

Let's start with the lady up front wearing the church hat. What's your name?

Lady: Karen

We have a Karen in the house! This is your question, is Abacavir a location or medication?

Lady: *(after a couple of seconds of thought)* "That's a magic word."

(Jesus laughs.)

You're confusing that with ABRACADABRA.

Lady: "OK, I'll say location."

(Jesus makes a loud buzzing sound.)

That is incorrect.

Who wants to go next? How about the guy in the back? What is your name?

Guy: "Jésus."

I like it, but you pronounce it differently than I do. You ready? Is Dothan a location or medication?

Guy: I think it's a place.

You are correct.

(Jesus tosses him a t-shirt.)

Let's do one more. How about someone sitting at that table of 20-somethings? I must say that I'm so happy to see so many young people here tonight. This is for the young lady with the blue hair. Is Scythopolis a location or medication?

(She looks to her friends for help.)

You can't phone a friend, that's a different game.

Young lady: "It sounds like something I ate at the Mediterranean restaurant last night. I'm going to guess. Is it a location?"

You are correct, here is your shirt.

Let me point out that we will be selling these shirts after the show. One hundred percent of the proceeds go to charity. I suspect they will be in high demand. Keep in mind what Matthew said in 5:40: "If anyone wants to… take your shirt, let him have your coat too." So it might be a good idea to buy two of them.

As we approach the end of the show it may be a good time to let you know my thoughts about church and comedy shows. They both should have the same goal. You should leave them feeling happier when you exit than when you walked in. They both should raise your spirits.

Nothing raises the spirit more than children and prayer. A child's innocence is refreshing, especially when they have questions. Have you ever noticed that a child who is laughing and smiling has remarkable power when it comes to making others happy?

I really enjoy listening to children tell me Bible stories. My favorite is when they tell me about Jonah. Sometimes they get their stories mixed up. They always get the whale part right, but sometimes they get Jonah mixed up with Geppetto. Most of the children know that lying is a sin, so it makes sense to them that Pinocchio would also be in the Bible with either Jonah or Geppetto. They recall Pinocchio and Jonah building a fire in the whale's belly. The smoke makes the whale sneeze and that releases them from captivity.

When I press the children for details about where they got the wood and matches for the fire, they are very creative. The best response I got was when I was told that Pinocchio would keep telling lies so his nose would grow. They would break off pieces of his nose to use as firewood. After they had enough firewood, Pinocchio would tell two more lies so they could break off two more pieces of wood to rub together and start a fire.

Let me tell you about this little boy who went to church. During the sermon he noticed that the preacher repeated things multiple times. He would say, "Are you filled with the Spirit? Are *you* filled with the Spirit? Are you filled with the *spirit*? Can I get an amen? Let me hear an amen. Give me an *AMEN!*"

After church the boy asked his dad, "Why does the preacher keep repeating himself"? His dad replied, "I don't know, maybe he thinks we are deaf." The boy went to ask his mom the same question. She replied, "Because the preacher knows that men don't listen, so he has learned to repeat himself when he wants to make a point."

Speaking of the Holy Spirit, there is a story about a little boy who was introduced to John 16:7 in Sunday school, after which he was convinced that John had a parakeet named Holy Spirit.

I've heard some of you use the phrase, "Jesus, Mary and Joseph" when you are upset or frustrated. Come on now, you know you've said it. To be frank, the phrase is not one of my favorites. I know some of you have modified it to "Cheese and Crackers," and I applaud you for that. I have to admit, it makes me smile when I hear children re-modify it to "Jesus Crackers." I can tell you that God smiles when he hears a child refer to communion as Jesus Crackers.

Matthew 6:9-13 tells us: "Pray then like this: Our Father in heaven, hallowed be your name. Your kingdom come, your will be done, on earth as it is in heaven. Give us this day our daily bread, and forgive us our debts, as we also have forgiven our debtors. And lead us not into temptation, but deliver us from evil."

This prayer does not have to be prayed word for word. It's all about intent. I've heard children pray it with the following verbiage, and it is just as effective.

"Our Father Art in Heaven, Harold be thy name. Thy kingdom come, thy wildebeest named Don, on earth and in heaven. Give us this day our jelly bread, and forgive us our bus passes, as we forgive those who pass us. Lead us not into Penn Station but deliver us from evil. Amen."

I want to leave you with Proverbs 3:6: "Seek God's will in all you do, and he will direct your paths."

Good night and God is blessing all of you.

(The MC takes the stage.)

MC: Give it up for Jesus Christ.

(Crowd erupts into applause and cheers.)

(The MC then acknowledges Jay Boc.)

> **Just a reminder that Jay's book, *Dads Cry Too* is available for sale along with t-shirts that say, "Tell me about your Dugong."**
>
> **And Jesus will be signing his book. If you have to ask which book, you have not been paying attention.**

CLOSING INTERVIEW IN THE GREEN ROOM

Me: **So how do you think it went?**

Jesus: I'm pretty happy with it. Some things need to be polished up a bit. I forgot to do some jokes, and I may have to move a couple things around. Maybe find a way to work in some more scripture.

Me: **For example?**

Jesus: The game show needs improving. I like the Dugong message but I'm kicking around something called Heaven's Sevens. The contestants would be asked to name the 7 Deadly Sins.

Avarice
Envy
Gluttony
Lust
Pride
Sloth
Wrath

Another question might be, "Name the 7 Virtues."

Justice
Fortitude
Prudence
Temperance
Faith
Hope
Charity

This one may be a little tougher. "Name the 7 days of Creation."

Monday, Tuesday, Wednesday, Thursday, Friday, Saturday, and Sunday are incorrect, but I'm willing to bet someone would answer that way.

The correct answer is:

Created Heaven and Earth: day and night
Divided Heaven from earth
Created the land, the sea, and vegetation

Created the sun, the moon, and the stars
Created creatures great and small
Created mankind
Sanctified the seventh day as a day of rest

This one may stump most people. "Name the 7 Medieval Champions of Christendom."

St. George, England
St. Denis, France
St. James, Spain
St. Anthony, Italy
St. Andrew, Scotland
St. Patrick, Ireland
St. David, Wales

How about the 7 gifts of the Holy Spirit?

Wisdom
Understanding
Counsel
Fortitude
Knowledge
Piety
Fear of the Lord

What do you think of this one? The 7 Spiritual Works of Mercy.

To convert the sinner
To instruct the ignorant
To counsel those in doubt

To comfort those in sorrow
To bear wrongs patiently
To forgive injuries
To pray for the living and the dead

And let's not forget about the 7 Corporal Works of Mercy.

To tend to the sick
To feed the hungry
To give drink to the thirsty
To clothe the naked
To harbor the stranger
To minister to prisoners
To bury the dead

On second thought, maybe I'll pass this on to St. Peter and he can make it an entrance exam for Heaven. The person arrives at the pearly gates. Once there St. Peter has them spin a wheel. Whatever question the spinner stops at is presented to the deceased. If they get it right… they get in. Get it wrong, well I have not thought it all the way through yet, but you see where I'm going.

Me: **Which jokes did you skip?**

Jesus: I wanted to dive in a little more on the topic of human struggle and frailty. I'm sure you already know that we are all made in the image of God. Ephesians 2:10 says "For we are his workmanship." However, it is readily apparent that God made some of us with spare parts. Who knows why? Maybe there was a supply chain issue. Maybe he just wanted to drop a hint about *His* sense of humor. Sometimes he puts the most unlikely people in our lives. There is a reason we have a saying that goes, "opposites attract." Sometimes people are put in our lives to make us better people, and sometimes it's because God wanted to laugh.

Or maybe I would have added something like this.

Have you ever noticed how often Weight Watchers is mentioned in the Bible? It's not mentioned by name but rather as "fasting." I would like to point out that the difference between fasting and feasting is just one letter. When fasting, it should not be in a showy fashion. Feasting should be festive. Feasting and festive have many of the same letters. God wants you to be festive.

Have you ever noticed that heavy people are often referred to as jolly or jovial? It's pretty rare to see sad people at a buffet. Las Vegas and Golden Corral have made an art of making people happy with a buffet. They take all of your money and make it up to you with a coupon for a free buffet. The next time you are considering fasting, stop and think, *Maybe God meant me to feast. Maybe fast and feast got mixed up in translation.*

Me: **Anything else?**

Jesus: I have some more material about the Apostles, disciples, and followers. I have a bit more of a routine about my cousin John, who baptized me, and lots of followers. Some people are surprised when I tell them that he was Jewish. They think he was a Baptist. This is where it turns into an Abbott and Costello routine.

Me: Meet my cousin John the Baptist.

Stranger: So he's a Baptist?

Me: Yes, but he's Jewish.

Stranger: Oh, so he converted to being a Baptist.

Me: No, he's a Jew who baptizes.

Stranger: I get it. He's a Jewish Baptist.

Let's talk about Patron Saints. I was at the mall today with Anthony of Padua. For those who don't know, he's the saint people pray to when they can't find lost items. We got separated while shopping, I looked all over the mall and I could not find him. I thought it was pretty ironic that I lost Saint Anthony.

As a public service announcement, some of you need to be reminded to dig up the Saint Joseph statues after the house is sold. There are a lot of upside-down statues in front yards, thinking this is the longest escrow *ever*.

There are Patron Saints that can be prayed to for a variety of reasons and causes. You might think that Saint Paul would be the Patron Saint of the Post Office. It makes sense when you realize how many letters he wrote. The reality is, he is the Patron Saint of people afflicted with carpal tunnel.

Paul wrote several letters to the Corinthians and makes several good points in them. In addition to addressing how we all are stewards of God's mysteries, he talks about working in the Spirit of God. All worthy points that should be addressed. However, the Bible failed to mention the part where Paul complimented the Corinthians about their excellent leather products. It took 2000 years, Ricardo Montalban, and the

Chrysler Cordoba to make us aware of "Fine Corinthian Leather."

Every time I see someone running, it reminds me that every saint has a past, and every sinner has a future. I can't help but wonder if that person is running *to* someone or *from* something? It also got me thinking about Proverbs 28:1. The wicked flee when no one pursues. That's why I don't jog. It's also hard to run in sandals.

If you don't mind, can I run a couple more things past you?

Me: **Absolutely, I would be honored.**

Jesus: Have you ever noticed that you can't spell devil without the letters in evil? And you can't spell good without the letters in God.

Jay Boc and I were talking before the show, and he was telling me how he fought off evil in his old age. He said he fights evil with the strength of God. He said he once stabbed a vampire with a wooden rake handle, beat zombies to death, and killed the devil himself. I gently pulled him aside and told him he was supposed to hand out candy to them on Halloween.

Speaking of the devil, I'm sure you know that the devil lost a gold fiddle to a young man in Georgia, but did you know his favorite flavor is sin-o-man?

Or, how about this one. Who was the worst financial person in the book of Exodus? Jochebed, she threw away a little (profit) prophet!

Me: **Did any of your fans say anything unexpected to you after the show?**

Jesus: Oh yeah. A young lady came up to me after the show and told me that she was a Social Influencer. She asked if I was more of a Social Influencer or a Moral Influencer. She followed that up by asking what my full-time job would be nowadays.

I told her that there is no way that I would be a Life Coach or a Social Influencer. I feel that those jobs are held by people who can't get... and hold down... a *real* job. I did point out that my BRAND is love, I'm on all platforms and have over 2 BILLION followers.

I might take a job in a coffee shop. But it would not be Starbucks! Maybe a place called Hebrews.

And there is always my carpentry background. Most people don't know that Joseph and I talked about going into business together. He thought Joseph and Son Carpentry was a catchy name. I liked Jesus and Dad better. Eventually he started a business with my siblings called the Nazarene Nailers.

Me: **Sounds like you have lots of material that you didn't get to, or may want to perfect for the next show. What is your first order of business?**

Jesus: PRAYER.

Me: **One more thing. Will you bless me?**

Jesus: COME!

CROSS REFERENCES

Chapel in the Woods in Michigan

Largest Crucifix in the World in Michigan

Nazarene pallet cross in Medina, Ohio

Sedona Cross in Arizona

Wendy's Cross. This photo was taken by Wendy Guerrero after a California wildfire. The church was gone but the cross still stood.

The end

ABOUT THE AUTHOR

Brian O'Connell is retired and lives in a small town 45 miles south of Cleveland, Ohio. He typically spends his time with his grandsons when he is not performing comedy at senior centers and church events. He is often considered one of the best clean comedians in the country. He rarely flies and has earned the nickname "The John Madden of comedy," therefore his engagements are usually limited to the Midwest and the East coast.

Brian is a techno-idiot who rarely checks his email (jbrianoconnell@gmail.com) for messages. It is not uncommon for him to intentionally leave his house for long periods of time without his cell phone. It is no wonder you may not have heard of him. His lack of flying, not being logged in, and forgetting his phone, make him a well-kept secret to many.

Brian is a typical grandfather whose best times are moments spent with his grandsons and helping at church functions. The not-so-typical part of Brian is that he is a former Hollywood stuntman, actor, comedian, author (*Dad's Cry Too*, available on Amazon), repo man, and bill collector.

Connect with the author:

Brian O'Connell
8796 Westfield Road
Seville, OH 44273

jbrianoconnell@gmail.com

www.ingramcontent.com/pod-product-compliance
Lightning Source LLC
Chambersburg PA
CBHW072134070526
44585CB00016B/1665